WORLD-WIDE CONCERT
BOOK

LIVE
AID

WORLD-WIDE CONCERT BOOK

LIVE AID

PETER HILLMORE

JFK Interviews by William McGuire

INTRODUCTION BY

BOB GELDOF

The Unicorn Publishing House
New Jersey

Published in the United States of America and
Canada by
The Unicorn Publishing House, Inc.,
1148 Parsippany Boulevard, Parsippany, NJ 07054

Published in the United Kingdom by
Sidgwick & Jackson Ltd
1 Tavistock Chambers, Bloomsbury Way,
London WC1A 2SG

Special thanks to Pixie Esmonde, Joe Dera,
Nicole Packer, Kevin Mazur, Bill Graham, Jane
Gregory, Kerry Hood, Larry Magid, Allen Spivak

Printing history
    10 9 8 7 6 5 4 3 2 1

Produced by Shuckburgh Reynolds Ltd
289 Westbourne Grove
London W11 2QA

Copyright © 1985 Xylopark Limited

Designed by Laurence Bradbury and Roy
Williams with help from Lucy Adams, Paula Coles,
Sarah Collins, Lesley Cook, David Fordham, Alun
Jones, Sylvia Kwan, Dinah Lone, Michael
McInnerney, Chris Meehan, Anita Plank, Roger
Pring, Sue Rawkins, Tessa Richardson-Jones,
Michelle Stamp, Sally Ward

Cover design by David Fordham

Photographs by Mohamed Amin, Brian Aris,
AT&T, Band Aid Trust, Adrian Boot, Laurence
Bradbury, British Telecom, Andrew Catlin, Ann
Clifford, Allen Davidson, Chalkie Davies, Fox
Keystone, Mike Fuller, Harrison Funk, Frank
Griffin, Allen Grisbrooke, Bob Gruen, John
Hoffman, Dave Hogan, Nils Jorgenson, Barbara
Kinney, Neil Leifer, Kevin Mazur, David
McGough, Tony McGrath, Paul Natkin, Denis
O'Regan, Neal Preston, Duncan Raban, Steve
Rapport, Ken Regan, Rex Features, Ebet Roberts,
Roy Williams, Richard Young, Vinnie Zuffante

Typeset by SX Composing Ltd and Optic
Typesetting
Printed and bound in Spain by Printer Industria
Grafica SA DLB 30225-1985

Library of Congress Cataloging in Publication
Data
Hillmore, Peter
    Live Aid

    1. Live Aid (Festival : 1985 : Philadelphia, Pa.,
and Wembley, Middlesex)   2. Rock musicians –
Pictorial works.   I. Title.
ML3534.H56   1985   784.5'4'007942185
85-16511
ISBN 0-88101-024-3 (alk.paper)

Origination by Printer Industria Grafica SA with
Scitex Response 350

CONTENTS

INTRODUCTION

I can remember a blur. Things that skitter in and out of the mind leaving a vivid image of happiness and . . . (I think) relief.

I saw little. I haven't even seen the videos. I watched Bowie, The Who, U2 and some others. I ran around between the TV trucks, the stage, the appeals office, the studio, the private box. I had a sore back, I was worried, I was eating a B.L.T. sandwich and . . . the noise. Jesus the noise.

A monstrous emotional bellow of support, goodwill, exuberance and true joy.

I remember walking on stage and all the bollocks of the previous weeks being flushed right down the ol' mental bog.

All that emotion directed at YOU.

The numb continuum I had been operating under washed away and the sheer romance and hugeness assaulting you. I live that moment now.

It was the first time I realized what had been unleashed.

The mike going dead and I didn't care and 80,000 people sang for me.

I remember 'Let It Be'. I can't believe it still. Me on stage singing with Bowie, Townshend and McCartney for God's sake.

I had been asleep seconds before. John Hurt and David Bowie woke me. John said 'Are you O.K?' David said 'C'mon we're on . . . do you know the words?' Strange, strange stuff.

Rehearsing 'Feed The World'. In the dark and only being able to tell who was singing by recognizing the voices. And then the end.

I look around and tears are pouring down the faces of this collection of men and women. Sounds corny doesn't it . . . it wasn't.

Even journalists cried. Thousands cried, millions cried. For those who were dying and for themselves. For whatever it was they had lost through the sheer crap of living and had rediscovered in a fleeting moment of clarity.

For a brief, brief moment – everything seemed possible.

The New Brutalism vanquished.

If there is a meanness, an empty cynicism, a terrifying selfishness and greed in us, then that day, watching that television, dancing in that crowd, playing on that stage, the obverse side of our cruelty was made manifest.

In an almost preposterous display of bravura, the world linked itself tangibly and physically in technological communion.

I was aware of people on every continent actively watching, willing it on, helping, on phones giving. Could you feel it?

I am gushing. But that is the only response. It happened. It did happen. I had wanted money. Thank you all – we got that. More than I had ever dreamed possible.

We had wanted governments to react. They were forced to. Next day Parliament in Britain debated. Money was given. The R.A.F. were allowed to keep their crucial airlift in Ethiopia, and politicians left for Africa to see for themselves what it was that had made people behave in such an unexpected manner.

In America talk of massive airlifts, food, emergency measures, congressional committees activated.

In Russia a desperate attempt to defend a record of cynicism, deceit and arms sales.

In Europe a plea to act. Finally.

But there was more, much more than that.

We were for a few hours no longer obsessed by ourselves. There was a misery greater than whatever personal nonsense we had to deal with. There was a desire to help – to do SOMETHING. It was so pathetically obvious that in a world of surplus, starvation is the most senseless death of all.

The politicians were humbled. Their ceaseless bickering seemed so small and irrelevant. Their inability to act or represent in any way this untapped compassion, understanding and generosity is to their everlasting disgrace. How much indeed are they responsible by their behaviour and demeanour and language for the loathing and mistrust they engender and the divisiveness they perpetrate.

What would be possible if we could be like July 13 1985 all the time?

Who will speak up for selflessness?

Anyway . . .

Please remember this day all of your lives. It's important.

Remember the day you wanted to help.

Remember the bands and crews who did it. The professionals who made it an extraordinary technological feat.

Remember the dying who were allowed to live.

Remember on the day *you* die, there is someone alive in Africa 'cos one day you watched a pop concert.

Remember your tears and your joy.

Remember the love.

Remember on that day for once in our bloody lives WE WON.

Remember that even though it's over, it need not stop.

Remember the dying goes on and remember so that as time passes you can tell others 'It's possible, I know'.

What a day, what a lovely day.

Bob Geldof
July '85.

WE ARE THE WORLD

There may never be a concert like it again. Never again scenes like the ones we saw on July 13, 1985. The day we tried to Feed The World.

Imagine, or remember, for a moment, the stage at the JFK stadium in Philadelphia. It is 11 o'clock at night; 16 hours after Status Quo, far away in London, began the day with 'Rocking All Over The World' ('it seemed the right song to start things off').

Bob Dylan is just finishing his last song. Behind him are two laconic guitar players, strumming out the rhythm. They are the Rolling Stones' Keith Richard and Ronnie Wood. The crowd, who have been locked into position since early morning roars its appreciation at the trio. A fitting finale – but it's just the beginning.

Lionel Ritchie comes out from behind the curtain, hugs Dylan, Richard and Wood, and waves to the crowd. The crowd waves back. And the curtains open, to reveal a crowded area, crowded with stars who normally occupy the whole stage themselves.

Ritchie begins to sing 'We Are The World, We Are The Children', and an excited roar comes from the crowd. Then Harry Belafonte joins in, followed by Joan Baez, and then Madonna. Then the tiny, devilishly pure voices of a choir of children are heard. The stage is full, crowded with rock stars, all singing together. Or trying to sing together – it's been a long, hot day, who really cares about the odd wrong note? There's Duran Duran, with the individual members of the group scattered about. There's Mick Jagger; he doesn't seem to know all the words but is singing to himself, dancing with himself, happy with himself ('I came for the cause, but I also came to enjoy myself').

Then Patti LaBelle, Tina Turner, Teddy Pendergrass and Dionne Warwick sing individual vocal bits, while the world's most priceless and talented chorus hums, sings, claps, smiles. There's been a hurried rehearsal, out backstage among the trailers, but no one worries if things get a bit haywire. This isn't a song, it's a celebration. Phil Collins is jumping around ecstatically; he's sung at both Wembley and Philadelphia, crossing the Atlantic in Concorde – 'Why? Because I'm mad, that's why. The whole day's mad.' The madness is contagious; Bob Dylan is hugging Robert Plant, Bryan Adams is hugging Jimmy Page. Everyone is hugging each other. Eric Clapton is hugging himself, because there's no one else left to hug.

The madness has spread to the crowd. Exhausted by the day and the heat, they are filled with energy again. A two-way drip feed of adrenalin has been set up between the stage and the audience. Each is fuelling the other with power. They, too, are singing. As the performers on the stage break into an encore (this will be the first time the concert overruns in 16 hours), 90,000 hands punch the air towards the stage. In celebration. In thanks. At that moment everyone feels like the world, and everyone behaves like children, aware that 1.5 billion people have watched them all around the globe, all day, and are probably punching the air in celebration at home.

They certainly were in England. Wembley Stadium had closed hours ago, its part in Live Aid complete. It was already July 14 in London; but all the stars had gathered in a London night club to watch the rest of the Philadelphia proceedings on television. No one wanted to sleep. That could come later. And as they watched, they remembered the good time, the celebration, the Finale they had had themselves a few hours earlier.

It had been hot at Wembley as well: the weather and the music. The crowd had just watched the Thompson Twins and Nile Rodgers on the satellite feed from America. Then Freddie Mercury and Brian May had come on to sing a quietly reflective song that reminded everyone of the real purpose of the day – 'Just think of all the hungry mouths we have to feed . . .'

The stage was empty, except for the piano that Elton John had left behind. The spotlight picked up a small slight figure as he walked to the piano – Paul McCartney. For many, for most of the audience, it was to be the first time they had heard a Beatles number sung live by a Beatle, as McCartney struck the opening chords of 'Let It Be'.

And then his microphone packed up. It was the kind of moment that could have ruined things – but in fact it was a moment that topped everything. As the crowd realized what was happening, as they watched the giant television screens that carried the image of his mouth moving soundlessly, 72,000 voices sang the song for him, until his microphone was restored. And then another great roar goes up, for a quartet of backing vocalists that ambles shyly into position by the piano. They're David Bowie, Alison Moyet, Pete Townshend – and Bob Geldof. They sing along with the 72,000. Then the entire British Live Aid contingent of performers fills the stage to sing 'Do They Know It's Christmas?' the song that started it all off, all those months, all those lives ago. There's The Who, who got together again especially for Live Aid ('God, it was strange playing

again before an audience,' confesses Townshend); there's Sting, his immaculate whites that he performed in seven hours ago now looking a little wilted. There's Bryan Ferry (somehow, he manages still to look immaculate); there's Queen, there's Spandau Ballet, Howard Jones, Elton John, Wham!, Style Council, U2, everyone who has performed on that day, July 13. No one has left the stadium. Not on a day like this.

Suddenly, Paul McCartney and Pete Townshend hoist Bob Geldof on to their shoulders. The three artists punch the air in triumph with their fists, and the audience do the same. They are all performers in the Live Aid show. Everyone is swaying and singing in rapture. There's been no real rehearsal for this finale, and Bob Geldof has predicted 'it might be a bit of a cock-up. But if you're going to cock it up, it's best to do it with billions of people watching.' But it isn't a cock-up. It's wonderful. It's July 13, 1985.

It's also a success. Musically, of course it was a success. It couldn't fail to be, not with that line-up, not with that talent. But it's also achieved a far, far greater purpose – by the time Live Aid is finally over, the roadies have finished packing up the gear, and the television satellites have been switched off, over £50 million ($70 million) has been pledged to Band Aid's Ethiopian fund by people all over the world. For that was what July 13, 1985, was all about.

Overleaf: Pages 10-11. Wembley finale; pages 12-13. JFK finale.

AN AMAZING DAY

Even before the day started, it was already an amazing day. Outside the huge gates of Wembley Stadium, groups of fans had gathered, camping out for the night to secure the best positions. One of them, 17-year-old Sharon Craig from Worcestershire, remembers the night 'as one long party, with people singing and getting excited. We knew something great was going to happen.' There was even a girl from America – she'd been unable to buy a ticket for Philadelphia, so she'd come to England and bought one for Wembley. It was the same concert after all, so what difference did a few thousand miles make?

In Philadelphia, people had started gathering at 4.30 on Friday afternoon to wait for the great day. Through the night, over 10,000 were to fill the parking lots outside JFK. The police reported no incidents.

Inside the stadiums, it wasn't quiet either. The huge revolving stages had been built, identical in each place. The giant Diamond Vision screens – to show giant pictures of the performers on stage to all parts of the stadium, as well as screen the acts from across the ocean and across the world – were blank. Row upon row, tier upon tier of empty seats, a huge empty expanse of ground, waiting for the fans.

But still there was noise, as technicians worked through the night,

The hottest ducats in town.

Camping out at JFK.

Wembley. Early Saturday morning.

making last-minute adjustments to the sound system, moving the banks of lights, shouting to, or maybe shouting at, the television people who were worrying about their satellite feeds. Workmen kept sticking down white tape on the stage to hide final alterations and urgent carpentry.

Dawn broke on July 13. The sun shone in Philadelphia and, after the worst rain-filled summer for years, it

Sixty minutes to Wembley showtime...

...and at JFK, Philadelphia.

Last minute preparation.

Checking the stage revolutions.

Phil Collins and Sting backstage.

Spandau Ballet's Gary Kemp.

The Hard Rock Café, backstage.

shone at Wembley too. Outside the stadiums, the bleary-eyed fans end their night-long parties and wait for the doors to open, ready to make the long dash to the front of the arenas, to secure the best view of the stage.

Inside, the technicians relax for a while. All they can do now is wait until things go wrong. Bob Geldof arrives at Wembley with his girl friend, Paula Yates and their little daughter, Fifi Trixi-Belle. After months and weeks of work his face looks permanently haggard, as if he is wearing 'Fatigue' by Max Factor. 'This is it', he says looking around him, 'this is The Day'. He kisses Paula for reassurance.

Backstage, the pace gradually increases; catering supplies are brought in. At Wembley, the Hard Rock Café has built a tented replica of its London restaurant to provide food for the performers (it's free, but there are huge tubs to put money in, and everyone does). Neither backstage area is smart or glamorous; just a collection of trailers, portable cabins and a few tables and chairs.

The stars may all be performing for free, but they have all been asked to make an even bigger sacrifice – they have had to leave their egos at home. As Gary Kemp, of Spandau Ballet, said wonderingly later in the afternoon: 'Usually, when we come off stage, there are people waiting with towels, drinks, all sorts of things. Here, I fell over, and no one gave a toss.'

Pinned up to each trailer and cabin door are notices, hastily written in felt pen. These give the precise time that each act is allowed to use the dressing room, before they must vacate it for the next act. The stages have three lights on them: green means five minutes left of the act; amber, two minutes; and when the red light flashes it means finish promptly, at once. Today the stage is no place for prima donnas.

Then the gates to the stadiums open. From the stage can be seen, from a long way off, first one person, then another, then lots suddenly appear at the other end of the giant arenas, all running.

U2's Bono, walking to work.

The Cars' Ric Ocasek arrives at JFK.

Supplies for a long, hot day.

The fanfare arrives.

They run for what seems like ages, slowly getting bigger. Until they reach the area in front of the stage, a place they have no intention of quitting for the whole of the day. It has begun.

Stars also begin arriving backstage. It doesn't matter that some of them will have to wait hours before they appear. They have come to hear and see the concert as well as perform. They too want to be part of the audience. They are as excited as the fans, for they are fans too. 'There are many of my heroes here today,' says Adam Ant, 'people I've worshipped from afar.'

It's not long before everywhere in the stadiums is crowded, and everywhere people are in good spirits. The normally taciturn security guards helpfully spray the crowds with water, to keep them cool (the police in both Wembley and Philadelphia later reported a bare handful of arrests, all minor).

An hour before the concert is due to start, Prince Charles and Princess Diana arrive at Wembley to meet the stars. The 24-year-old Princess is a rock fan, and she is clearly excited to be introduced to people whose records she plays in Kensington Palace. Then she takes her seat in the Royal Box, the future Queen sitting in front of members of the present-day Queen – John Deacon and Roger Taylor. David Bowie acts as courtier.

Charles and Diana arrived early, to meet the performers.

One trailer area in Philadelphia is especially crowded. Seven people are sitting round a table talking together – Eric Clapton, Jimmy Page, Robert Plant, Phil Collins, Ronnie Wood, Keith Richard and Bob Dylan. Plant is writing on a piece of paper: it is the words to 'Stairway To Heaven', a song he hasn't played for so long he's forgotten the words. When he goes on stage he places the paper where he can see it. Backstage at Wembley, two people clasp their arms around each other and then collapse laughing at some private joke – David Bowie and Paul McCartney.

At Wembley, the VIP section of the stadium is some way from the back-stage area, and the performers walk through the crowds to watch the concert. There's minimal protection, but they seem unconcerned, chatting to the fans. A quiet figure in white leans

The Prince of Wales meets Bob Geldof.

Whatever has Diana said?

against the wall at the back of the stand. It is Sting – 'this is what rock and roll is all about,' he says, watching the massive audience. 'It's an Event, as much as it's Music.'

One person who doesn't seem to have the time to walk anywhere is Bob Geldof who, in the end probably saw less of his concert, his day, than anyone else. He is forever running between various locations – interview rooms, television points, control boxes, even the restaurant to try and find his father, who got lost. When he saw Paul and Linda McCartney he literally fell into

David Bowie and Paul McCartney share a quip.

their arms. It could have been friendship, it could have been exhaustion.

In Philadelphia, the air conditioning has failed in one dressing room, a trailer slightly different from the rest. It is the one used by Teddy Pendergrass, who is making his first appearance since the accident that left him paralysed three years ago. Sitting in his wheelchair, the portable fans cannot stop his body from being bathed in sweat. The green fibreglass roof casts an eerie glow on his frame. He is nervous, but determined: 'I am very afraid for personal reasons. But at the same time it couldn't be for a better cause. We're trying to feed the hungry black children in Africa.' He receives a standing ovation when he goes on stage, and his voice takes on new strength.

Teddy Pendergrass.

Everybody who performed in Live Aid on that amazing day was famous. Well, almost everyone. Two people weren't. One may become famous – no one knows the name of the other.

The first is Bernard Watson, and he actually began Live Aid in Philadelphia; it started a few minutes earlier than scheduled because of him. He came from the JFK parking lot where he had lived for nearly a week, badgering promoter Bill Graham with a cassette of his work. Graham would send food out to Watson; and then the day before

the concert he thought 'Why Not?' and told Watson 'You'll start the whole thing off.' And so, at 8.52 Eastern Standard Time, eight minutes before the scheduled start, Bernard Watson started the Amazing Day.

The other person is a household name only in her own household. U2 were on stage at Wembley; suddenly the singer, Bono, slid 30 feet down the side of the stage, disappeared into the audience and reappeared with a girl from the crowd. He danced with her and gave her a smacking kiss. For a few moments, this unknown girl's face was seen by 1.5 billion people around the world. An Amazing Day.

JFK...

Wembley.

Beach Boy Mike Love.

Cliff Richard and Bob Geldof.

Bette Midler.

Freddie Mercury and Elton John.

Sade smiles.

Tom Petty and Robert Plant.

Cher reclines.

The Who sweat.

Tina Turner.

Stephen Stills and Jimmy Page.

Elton John and George Michael.

Mr and Mrs Elton John with George Michael in the Royal Box.

Howard Jones sits in the Wembley stands.

In the Royal Box.

David Bowie.

Jeff Bridges, Mrs Harry Chapin and Kenny Loggins at JFK.

Madonna and friends arrive at JFK.

From 'Woodstock', to JFK: Crosby, Stills and Nash.

The Spands' Tony Hadley and Roger Daltrey.

David Bowie and Freddie Mercury.

Mark Knopfler and Bob Geldof.

Tom Petty and Stephen Stills.

Keith Richard wipes the sweat from Jack Nicholson's chin. Bob Dylan looks on.

Jack Nicholson and Jim Kerr.

Pete Townshend and Hazel O'Connor.

Andrew Ridgeley.

Billy Connolly and Pamela Stephenson.

Nils Lofgren.

'Miami Vice' star Don Johnson, a compere at JFK, with his son.

The stars also come to watch – David Essex.

John Deacon and Sting.

Paul Young and Alison Moyet.

Joan Baez.

Rick Springfield.

Backstage small talk.

Queen and Adam Ant.

The day's nearly finished, and so is Geldof. His friend, Paula Yates, understands.

LIVE AID PEOPLE

Photographer Brian Aris set up a make-shift studio in a corridor at Wembley. Ken
Regan made similar arrangements at JFK. A selection of their work appears on the following pages.

A well known band at Wembley.

Ozzy Osbourne and Black Sabbath.

Tom Petty and the Heartbreakers.

REO Speedwagon.

Power Station.

The Beach Boys.

The Thompson Twins.

Simple Minds.

The Cars.

Pat Metheny and Santana.

Bryan Ferry.

Sting.

The McCartneys.

Patti LaBelle.

Madonna.

Crosby, Stills and Nash.

Bob Dylan.

Dire Straits.

The Who.

Queen.

Robert Plant, John Paul Jones, Jimmy Page.

The Four Tops.

George Thorogood, Bo Diddley, Albert Collins.

Bryan Adams.

The Pretenders.

Eric Clapton.

Duran Duran.

Ashford, Simpson, Teddy Pendergrass.

Hall and Oates.

Chevy Chase, Jack Nicholson, Joe Piscopo.

Noel Edmonds, Griff Rhys-Jones, Harvey Goldsmith, Bob, Mel Smith.

Phil Collins and Dave Gilmour.

Nik Kershaw and Adam Ant.

Bob, Paula and Fifi.

David Bowie with Wembley Live Aid programme.

THEY ARE THE CHILDREN

We are the world – they are the children. And the children are dying. They died on the plains and in the hills of Ethiopia even while the music blared out in the stadiums of Philadelphia and Wembley. And they are dying as you read this.

Live Aid may have been a triumph. But it was a triumph born out of a tragedy, the tragedy of famine, the tragedy of starvation. This was what the concert was all about: not about the pulsing, energetic music of rock and roll played by the world's greatest musicians, not about the wonders of technology that spanned the globe and united the continents – but about hunger. About hunger, about drought, about famine. About despair.

When Joan Baez opened the show in Philadelphia at 9am it was 4pm in Ethiopia. As she told the crowd that 'we will move a little from the comfort of our lives to understand their hurt', crowds of people in that country were experiencing hurt that we could perhaps understand – but it's too big a hurt for us to really comprehend.

In the Live Aid programme at Wembley, Bob Geldof wrote about a shattering trip he made to Ethiopia in the very early days of Band Aid: 'There is a child. I think maybe it's four months old. The doctor says: 'No, it's two years old.' It squats on baked mud, a tattered dusty piece of cotton hangs from one

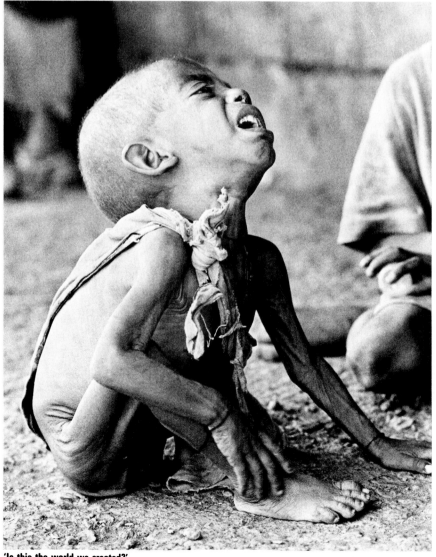

'Is this the world we created?'

Dawn of another long, hungry day.

There's a silence that goes with despair. There's no conversation worth making.

Waiting for food at a Red Cross centre.

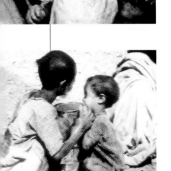

The television images that started it all.

shoulder on to its distended stomach. Its face is huge. A two-year-old face on a four-month-old body'.

Magnify that a hundred times – how do you comprehend it? Magnify it a thousand, a million times as you must in Ethiopia – how do you comprehend what the United Nations has called 'The greatest natural disaster faced by man'?

All the people who went to Live Aid, and most of the people who saw it on television, live in countries where governments spend more money on destroying food than Live Aid earned to buy food. Two months before the concerts, for example, Europe spent £265 million ($375 million) on destroying 2 million tons of food, when even one meagre Band Aid biscuit will keep a child in Ethiopia alive for 24 hours. How can you understand that?

It was in October 1984 that we were first forced to at least try to understand the horror of the latest hunger. People in their living rooms saw the first pictures of the dying in Ethiopia, a place where food or rain never seemed to come. The pictures were harrowing as

they showed a starving nation dying on its feet with a proud yet seemingly hopeless dignity. And all for want of food.

We were all moved, in Joan Baez's words, 'from the comfort of our own lives', and a good many dinners in Western homes went uneaten or tasted rather hollow, watching the report from the feeding centres of Korem and Makele, where there wasn't enough food.

Boomtown Rats' singer Bob Geldof was one of those who felt sick to his stomach at the sight of the distended bellies. The picture that moved him most was the sight of a nurse choosing 300 people to be fed from 10,000 who needed to be fed – 'what separated those chosen to live from those condemned to die was a waist-high wall. The people picked to be fed stood ashamed of their good fortune on one side of the wall, turning their backs in shame on the others. The ones left behind, in effect condemned to die, stood and watched with a beautiful dignity.'

Anxious, even desperate, to do

something, anything, Bob Geldof decided to try to make a record that would raise money for famine relief. Christmas was coming up in the Western world, the time of the year when we live in an atmosphere of giving, of plenty, of warmth, but a season that has no meaning when you're starving, close to death.

Band Aid was formed; Geldof and Ultravox's Midge Ure wrote 'Do They Know It's Christmas?/Feed The World'. Bob then set about contacting as many performers as he could to record the song. The response was overwhelming and enthusiastic. Within days, 40 top stars had agreed to perform; studios were lent, equipment was borrowed.

Sting remembers the formation of Band Aid very well: 'Bob rang me up almost immediately after he'd seen the television documentary. He'd already written a song with Midge, and he wanted to get other people to agree to be involved. I like Bob; he's known as "Bob the Gob" and I thought if anybody could do it he could, because of his extraordinary energy. So I said Yes. Then, in the following weeks, other people said Yes, and everyone wanted to be involved.'

And so, on November 25, 1984, recording history was made. An array of stars trooped up to a shabby recording studio: Sting, John Taylor, Martin Kemp, Boy George, Wham!, Style

How do you tell a baby there isn't any food?

Band Aid founders Midge Ure and Bob Geldof with Fifi.

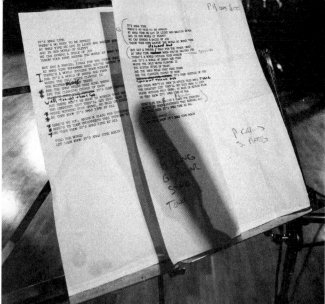

The song, hastily typed for the recording session.

Band Aid, November 25, 1984. 'Do They Know It's Christmas?'

THEY ARE THE CHILDREN

United Artists.

July 13, 1985 is Live Aid Day – officially.

Council, Bono, Gary Kemp, Phil Collins, Paul Young and many many more – the list read more like a hit-parade list in a music paper than a chorus line for a hastily assembled and hurriedly written record.

And that would be that, thought Geldof. It was estimated that the record would be able to tap the novelty and compassion market in equal measures, and achieve a modest success, £70,000 ($100,000) maybe, £100,000 ($140,000) if Band Aid was lucky. But the song was no novelty, and they severely underestimated the compassion that the Ethiopian famine had aroused (and the quality of the song). Within an hour of the record's release the original estimate had been reached, and the record went on to become the best-selling single of all time in the United Kingdom! It raised £8 million ($11 million) worldwide.

Something had happened, something had started, something that no one wanted to stop and that would eventually lead to the Live Aid show. In America, USA for Africa was formed and artists got together to record 'We Are The World, We Are The Children'. In Canada, in Australia, in Norway, everywhere where there were rock stars, there was a record.

The money that Band Aid raised had an immediate destination, and an immediate purpose – to buy and transport food. 150 tons of high energy biscuits were sent, 1,335 tons of milk powder, 560 tons of oil, 470 tons of sugar, 1,000 tons of grain. Money was sent to the relief agencies, and lorries and trucks were bought to transport the supplies.

Those figures may be impressive, but they're not enough; all they mean is that more people are chosen to live out of 10,000 – more than just 300. But now there are even more than 10,000 in every line. There is still so much that has to be done; not just to feed the hungry, but to provoke and refuel the outcry that would prod indifferent governments into action (Bob Geldof once had a memorable public argument with Britain's Prime Minister over aid.) because the prospects are still very grim indeed.

The Save the Children Fund says that 'what we saw last year is a pale shadow of the horror that is going on at the moment – and things are going to get considerably worse'. What is needed now is more money, lots more money. That's so much more important than sympathy and sorrow.

This ship saves lives.

Band Aid chartered three ships to transport food and supplies to Africa. They sail every single week.

The ships are loaded in London.

The end of the voyage.

Medicine, tents, jeeps, trucks, grain, flour, vegetable oil. They all save lives.

There's never enough supplies.

It is not enough just to feed people. They must be helped to start their lives again.

One of the few feeding stations in the drought hit areas of Ethiopia.

PLUGGING IN THE
GLOBAL JUKEBOX

It was one of those crazy ideas that people either laugh at or grin and say 'Why Not?' Bob Geldof visited America for the recording session, on January 28, of 'We Are The World', which furthered the Band Aid idea. In the studio he announced his intention of continuing the pop industry's gesture on a global scale.

We would, he said, 'telecast the world's biggest concert'. It would take place in England and America, 'on the same day in July'. It was a crazy idea, and people laughed. Anyone could realize, almost without thinking, that the problems would be immense and the cost huge. In the summer months, rock stars are all touring. You could never get them together in one place, or even two places, at the same time. Even Geldof wasn't sure he was being serious himself.

But as time progressed, and more money flowed into Band Aid's banks, saving more lives, he began to think 'Why Not?' Band Aid had kept millions alive, 'but now we must give them a life. And that needs money, lots of it, for long-term development projects. I'm a pragmatist – if there's a problem, you have to go out and solve it.'

If the musicians would agree, it would make a great show, the world's greatest. If he could get some stars to agree to perform, then others would feel reassured and come in as well. Working from the yellow living room of his house in Chelsea, London, Geldof began ringing everyone he knew.

Queen recall just how hard he hustled and cajoled. 'We were touring in the Far East at the time,' recalls their manager. 'He found out where we were staying in Japan and rang us. Then he found out where we were staying in Australia and rang us there. Finally, we

BOB GELDOF

Some people are born great, others achieve greatness – and some have greatness thrust upon them. With Bob Geldof, it's a mixture of the last two.

The 32-year-old Irish rock star who pleaded and cajoled, flattered and abused people into making records, appearing in concerts and saving lives in Ethiopia is the son of a Dublin merchant (his grandfather was a Belgian pastry cook who went to Ireland). His mother died when he was young and he was virtually brought up by his elder sister.

He was educated at a Catholic school, Black Rock College, and after casual jobs as a truck driver, busker, English-language teacher and factory hand, he went to Canada and worked as a pop music journalist on a Vancouver paper, the *Georgia Strait*.

In 1975 he returned to Dublin to go into the publishing business. He was about to launch his own free newspaper, when he joined some friends who were forming a rock group, the Boomtown Rats.

Their singles like 'Rat Trap' and 'I Don't Like Mondays' reached Number One in the charts.

Geldof lives with his girl friend, television presenter Paula Yates, and their daughter Fifi, in an old priory in Kent. And he saves lives in Ethiopia, Sudan and other parts of Africa.

The American promoters: Bill Graham and Larry Magid.

'The next time Bob has an idea, I'm going on holiday.' Harvey Goldsmith.

If I had stopped to think . . . I certainly would have said No – Harvey Goldsmith

got a call from him when we were in New Zealand.'

Mick Jagger remembers one meeting with Geldof, 'where he brought his dog, and Bob, the dog and I talked. After that meeting, I was up to doing it.' Jagger talked to David Bowie about doing something together (they would have sung together, one in Wembley, one in Philadelphia, but the four-second delay on the satellites ruled that out, so they made a video instead – and Jagger got together with Tina Turner).

After weeks of working with his address book, Geldof's idea began to take on a reality and a momentum of its own. It was still a pretty hair-brained scheme – a 16-hour concert, for heaven's sake, in two different continents on the globe. But people liked the idea. The musicians, the most important part, were enthusiastic. Crosby, Stills and Nash even decided to charter a jet to get them from their tour to wherever the concert would be held, if it came off.

Gradually, but slowly, the idea of a 'global jukebox' became more and more like reality, as more and more stars said 'Why not, Yes all right'. With the list of stars he had, at least 14 different schedules and timetables for performers were drawn up – and then thrown away, as new stars came in. Eric Clapton had agreed, so had Sting, Phil Collins, Spandau Ballet, Mick Jagger, David Bowie, Status Quo, Dire Straits, Queen, 45 groups in all with still more to come in later weeks. The Who decided to reunite and their decision was made only minutes before the actual concerts were publicly announced ('it was rather like getting one man's four ex-wives together', remembers Geldof).

There were, however, still frequent times when Geldof doubted whether it would all come off in the way he had first imagined it. 'Every day seemed to have its upside and its downside, every day had some new problem.' Some groups said 'Yes', and then pulled out for a variety of reasons, some understandable, some not. Geldof used all sorts of pressure to persuade groups to appear. 'I told them they could perform what they liked and how they liked; they could even do their act hanging from chandeliers if they wanted, as long as they appeared.'

It wasn't just the desire to give the crowds a good line-up that lay behind Geldof's constant pressurising. 'I reckoned that a lot of fans might watch the show on television mainly because their favourite group was appearing. If just 10 per cent of these then made a donation it was a lot more money for the Fund.' It was that simple an equation.

Now, the professional promoters could be called in and asked to donate their time and their skills. 'If I had stopped to think what Bob was suggesting when he walked into my office, I'd probably have laughed and I certainly would have said No', says Harvey Goldsmith, the leading British rock music promoter (he has asked Bob to let him know in advance if he has a similar idea, 'so I can book my holiday'). But Goldsmith didn't stop to think, American promoters were contacted, and the project was on. Just 35 days later, on July 13, 1985.

One of the American promoters, Larry Magid, recalls the terrifying frenzy of that final month, and, strangely enough its advantage: 'What

Bill Graham makes things happen right.

It all passed as a blur for Bob Geldof.

We're all looking for an honest person. Well, we've found one in Bob Geldof – Larry Magid, co-promoter

Building up to the day, at Wembley...

... and at JFK stadium, Philadelphia.

Preparing The Global Jukebox.

was great about the whole thing was the fact that we had only 35 days to pull the show off. Time was not a deterrent; it was actually an ally because you did not have any time to think what was going on. You just had to do it.'

And there was a lot that had to be done. Wembley was the obvious choice for the London venue: it's the most famous stadium in Britain, the site of major sporting events. It holds 72,000 people, and most important of all, was having a series of Bruce Springsteen concerts a week before Live Aid was scheduled, so there would be lots of equipment already in place.

In America, plans to use Shea Stadium in New York and then Washington D.C. came to nothing; the West Coast couldn't be considered because of the huge time difference with London. So the organisers chose the JFK stadium in Philadelphia. It holds 90,000, and has the largest backstage area of any stadium – no small

Bill Graham, with the artists' list.

The running order at Wembley.

point when you consider how many stars would be arriving. Even if they left their entourages at home, there would still be the huge trailers carrying the equipment. Stage companies, sound companies, lighting experts were all recruited for both stadiums.

It wasn't just a matter of putting on the world's greatest-ever concerts in the world's shortest possible time. It was also a case of trying to do it at the world's lowest cost – the cheaper it was to put on, the more profit went to Band Aid and the more money went to Ethiopia.

British Airways lent Band Aid the supersonic plane, Concorde, for the day, so that some stars could play in both Wembley and Philadelphia. Police were persuaded to give their services free. Expensive technology was provided at cost. Everyone who could be hustled was hustled. And everyone worked together. Top promoter Bill Graham says that usually American promoters 'are like the Mafia, with our own bit of territory. On this we all co-operated.' Helping Live Aid was an offer they couldn't refuse.

Filling both stadiums would be no problem; nearly any of the acts due to

British Telecom technology.

AT & T hardware from America.

perform could do that by themselves, let alone with the other performers. Sure, that would make a tidy profit for Ethiopia. But, when he first thought of the crazy idea, Bob Geldof had thought in terms of a telecast to the whole world, a global jukebox for the global village. Whatever the message of July 13, television would be the medium for that message.

The company that masterminded the coverage of the Los Angeles Olympics took charge of the television packaging. Sixteen satellites were commandeered to beam the concert almost everywhere in the world. It would be sent to almost any country that wanted to see it. The developing countries of Africa would get it free of charge, other countries would pay for it.

They would also do something for Africa, by organizing telephone appeals for cash at regular intervals throughout the concerts, asking, urging, ordering people to send money. The response and the excitement was total. In America and Britain the concert would be on television for at least 16 hours, every minute of it. People would see it from Iceland to Ghana. By the time July 13 came round, a total of 1.5 billion people were ready to see the show; or put another way, 85 per cent of the world's television sets would be tuned into Live Aid.

At one point Bob Geldof found himself talking earnestly to the head of the Norwegian telephone system, and he now knows more about the workings of the New Caledonian Postage Service than he ever thought he would. In Australia, Channel 9 had first agreed to televise the concerts, then very abruptly changed its mind. Another arrangement was terminated at almost the last minute because the station's plans for the all-important telephone appeal were woefully inadequate.

As the day grew nearer, the momentum grew irresistible. Australia announced it was going to have a 'mad Australian down-under day', Italy broached plans to have an opera singer sing with 500 rock stars, several countries asked if they could have a bit of air time.

By the time July 13 came round, Live Aid really was the World.

'If you're going to cock it up, you might as well do it in front of billions of people.'

THE CONCERT
JULY 13, 1985

Wembley, London.

Even if it were to go wrong, it could still claim to be the greatest show on earth. 1.5 billion people were ready to see it, in nearly every country where there were television sets.

Even if half the artists didn't turn up, it would still be the greatest line-up ever seen on one day. Almost every act was capable of headlining a capacity concert on its own. Here, there were no headliners. Everyone was a star, and everyone was a supporting act.

The line-up was priceless, but no one was getting paid. They had all agreed to perform for two reasons. The famine in Africa beggared the imagination but was a horrible reality for millions. The concert, or the money it would raise, would help alleviate a little of the suffering of those who

JFK, Philadelphia.

wouldn't hear it.

Second, the music industry has always had a reputation for being a 'Me, Me' industry; tantrums and excesses are commonplace – even among some of the stars appearing today. But, for this day at least, the industry could show what it could do for other people. For once, just once, perhaps for only one day, the industry's hyperbole would be excusable.

It wouldn't be two concerts, separated by thousands of miles. It would be one concert, joined by technology. The artists from other countries, who would only be seen on the television, who would not be in either stadium, were also part of the same concert. The world would be joined, because July 13 was the day we tried to feed it.

Hello, Are You All Right?
– Francis Rossi of
Status Quo.
Yes – 72,000 Wembley
fans

No one was looking at the stage when the greatest show on earth began at Wembley. All eyes were turned to the Royal Box as Prince Charles and Princess Diana entered to the sound of an unrocking fanfare of trumpets. Diana said she'd been to a Dire Straits concert earlier in the week, and Charles said he would buy 'a pair of denims'.

Then *Status Quo* began the real music with 'Rocking All Over The World' which is what we'd all be doing for the next 16 hours. Status Quo had said they would never play live again, but Geldof changed their minds. Diana sang along, and Charles tapped his brogues.

After their allotted 17 minutes (no one had any longer), they left the revolving stage, and on came *Style Council*. Paul Weller looked as if he'd had his hair cut specially for the occasion.

A last-minute switch in the timetable had been made to enable the Prince and Princess to hear *Bob Geldof* and *The Boomtown Rats*. 'This is the best day of my life,' says Geldof, and thousands of spectators agree. He may love this Saturday, but Geldof sings, 'I Don't Like Mondays'. When he finishes the line, 'and the lesson today is how to die', he pauses in silence for a few seconds. The crowd is hushed, too.

It may be the best day of his life, but The Rats get 17 minutes, and no more, before it's the turn of *Adam Ant*. 'The world is watching, let's feed it.'

Live Aid begins.

FANFARE

STATUS QUO

Rocking all over the world... Status Quo kicks off at Wembley.

Rick Parfitt.

THE STYLE COUNCIL

Paul Weller.

THE BOOMTOWN RATS

It was his idea. It's his day. All those people are there because of him. He deserves this moment. Ladies and gentlemen, Bob Geldof and the Boomtown Rats!

'And the lesson today is how to die...

'I can't do what you can do and you can't do what I can do. But we both have to do it' - Mother Theresa.

Charles and Diana join the crowd at Wembley.

Queen, Prince, Princess and Irishman.

Countdown to showtime.

ADAM ANT

INXS comes over on video.

There are many of my heroes here – people I've worshipped from afar – Adam Ant

ULTRAVOX

'If two tossers from Ireland and Scotland can get off their butts and do something, maybe other tossers will do the same' – Midge Ure.

LOUDNESS

Midge Ure wrote 'Do They Know It's Christmas?' with Geldof, and helped start Live Aid.

It went very quickly. The greatest moment of my life, and it just flashed by! – Spandau Ballet's Gary Kemp

The man who wrote 'Do They Know It's Christmas?' with Geldof, Midge Ure, leads on *Ultravox*, who are playing live for the first time in nearly a year. It doesn't show as they increase the heat the audience are feeling by scorching through 'Dancing With Tears In My Eyes' and 'Vienna'. Ure seems very moved by the whole thing, but then it would be surprising if he wasn't, if anyone wasn't. . . .

Then it's the turn of Japan to make an international contribution. The satellites bring us, intermittently, top Japanese groups including *Loudness* which lives up to its name, even at that distance. Japan's other contribution is rather meagre – only £500,000 is raised for Africa.

Then with an entirely accurate yell of 'Hello World', Tony Hadley leads on *Spandau Ballet*, who start with 'Only When You Leave Me' and their set has the audience dancing. Gary Kemp thinks this is only fair, and he thanks the crowd for buying tickets 'and supporting the cause'.

Japan's video contribution, Loudness.

Pirouetting.

SPANDAU BALLET

Tony Hadley.

Steve Norman.

'The greatest moment of my life' – Gary Kemp.

Usually, when we come off stage, there are people waiting with towels, drinks . . . Here I fell over and no one gave a toss – Gary Kemp

We will move a little from the comfort of our lives to understand their hurt – Joan Baez

The Philadelphia concert starts a few minutes before the official opening time, with an unknown, *Bernard Watson*, who camped out in the stadium's parking lot for a week, begging the promoters to let him sing. Then *Joan Baez* performs the first 'official' number, and goes on to give the 90,000 crowd some pretty heavy preaching about the concert's message; no one seems to mind. Then it's the turn of *The Hooters* who get the crowd pretty excited.

Elvis Costello comes on stage at Wembley carrying only his electric guitar. There is the first bit of community singing as the audience happily sing along to 'All You Need Is Love'. Then the satellites give us Austria's song for Ethiopia, 'Why?' sung by the country's top pop group, *Opus*.

Nik Kershaw reckons, with some justification, that '1.5 billion people is definitely the biggest audience I've ever played to'. He also claims to be pretty nervous, but it doesn't show as he sings 'Wouldn't It Be Good', which it is. Bob Geldof is being given pain-killers backstage for his bad back. When he is constantly seen with back bent, it is not an uncharacteristic sign of humility. It's pain.

Bernard Watson waiting outside for the big moment.

A day earlier, Bernard Watson was unknown.

BERNARD WATSON

JOAN BAEZ

Joan Baez.

ELVIS COSTELLO

Elvis Costello, one of the attractions.

HOOTERS/OPUS

The Hooters.

Especially while playing, we felt a part of an event that was really going to get something done for the cause – The Hooters

The land is scorched and misery knows no mercy, as usual,

Opus from Vienna.

NIK KERSHAW

Nik Kershaw sings 'Wouldn't It Be Good.

Philadelphia TV interviews Nik at Wembley.

B.B. King beamed live from The Hague.

I came here to play music, and I didn't really realize the full extent and magnitude of what it is all about. Now I'm here, it's just the greatest event ever – Ozzy Osbourne

The American actor and comedian, *Chevy Chase*, is on stage at Philadelphia, introducing the legendary *Four Tops*, who are there, in their words, because 'today all the racial issues are eliminated and we are all working for one issue and one issue alone – to help everyone who needs help.' Then Chase welcomes *Billy Ocean*, who responds to the energy the crowd are sending out to the performers on stage, 'the feeling ran right through my bones' (just like it was doing to Geldof's back).

In the world link-up it is the turn of Holland. But we do not get a local Dutch group, although we do get three exotically clad TV presenters; instead there's *B.B. King* playing live at the North Sea Jazz Festival.

At Wembley, it's the turn of singer *Sade* whose lilting voice floats gently and sweetly in the warm air, asking 'Why Can't We All Live Together?' and then, as if she's talking about the good humour of the jammed crowd, 'Your Love Is King'.

Then it's back to Philadelphia for *Ozzy Osbourne* and *Black Sabbath*, and the exotic heavy metal star, known for biting the heads off chickens (which he doesn't do today), makes an adroit contrast to Yugoslavia's contribution, via the satellite, *Yu Rock Mission*, composed of nearly all the country's pop stars (well, it doesn't have many) and lots of sweet youngsters.

Chevy Chase as compere.

The Four Tops.

THE FOUR TOPS / B.B. KING

BILLY OCEAN

Billy Ocean signs a shirt.

Billy Ocean.

OZZY OSBOURNE

Run DMC.

Yu Rock Mission on video.

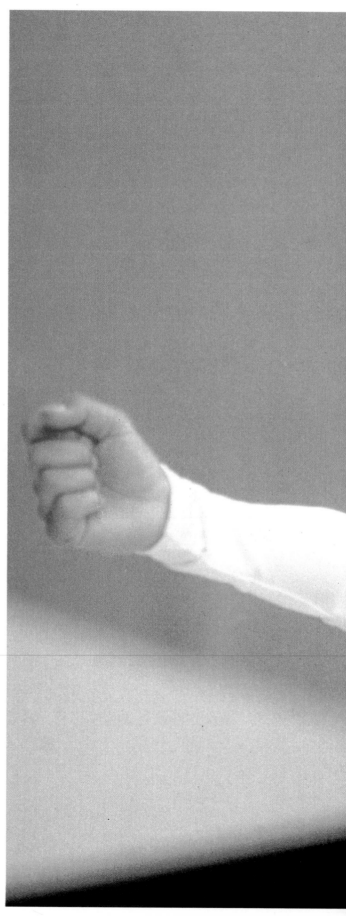

SADE

Why am I playing at both Wembley and Philadelphia? Because I'm mad, that's why – Phil Collins

British television personality and disc jockey, Noel Edmunds (who lent the organizers his helicopters to transport the stars to Wembley), introduces the new, and only for the afternoon, partnership of *Sting* and *Phil Collins*. Sting comes on first, tells everyone that 'Phil will be joining us in a minute' and then sings a solo version of The Police hit 'Roxanne'. He is accompanied by a cool saxophone, and then a cool piano joins in – with Phil Collins playing 'Against All Odds'. Both artists play solo numbers, each listening quietly on stage to the other. And then they team up to sing together, 'Long, Long Way To Go' and 'Every Breath You Take'.

In Philadelphia, *Rick Springfield* has been performing and declares the whole day ideal: 'For a musician the message is great; it's what we love, you can change the world with music.' That may or may not be true, no one knows if they're listening in the White House (we know they're not in the Kremlin). But we do get a change of music, when heavy metal band *REO Speedwagon* come on..

A shy, rather diffident voice tells the Wembley crowd, 'Hello, I'm just going to do a little song at the piano,' which is what *Howard Jones* proceeds to do. He also asks the crowd – or rather, he politely says, 'I'd really appreciate it' – to sing along in the chorus bits. The crowd does so.

Sting.

Howard Jones and Sting backstage.

STING

Audience participation.

Security.

RICK SPRINGFIELD

LI

PHIL COLLINS

What's 3½ hours of
flying? I'm just glad to be
involved – Phil Collins

REO SPEEDWAGON

REO Speedwagon.

HOWARD JONES

Howard Jones.

To get the Four Tops, Crosby, Stills and Nash, and Judas Priest on the same stage, on the same day, within the same hour – it's incredible – Judas Priest

The satellites take everybody in Philadelphia and Wembley live to Moscow, where the Russian pop group *Autograph* perform a mixture of family and progressive music. People agree that Russian pop groups sound a little, er, unliberated, but it's nice to have them with us, today.

By this time the spectators at Wembley have been listening to music for over four hours. Just in case people are wilting, *Bryan Ferry* comes on with an army of backing musicians and proceeds to have himself a ball, tear the roof of the stadium off (if it had one, that is) and to get people dancing about with renewed energy.

In Philadelphia, *Crosby, Stills and Nash* are on stage; the trio altered their schedule and chartered a plane to be at Live Aid – because, explains Graham Nash, 'I'm a person, just like you. Rock star, pop star, who cares?'

Despite a long, heavy, political speech live from Cologne, before *Udo Lindenberg* blasts out his song on the giant Diamond Vision screens dotted around both stadiums, the crowds are loving it. Security guards spray the fans with hoses, buckets and house-plant sprayers, in an effort to keep them cool. Security guards being helpful? It's a weird kind of day.

But it's hard to stay cool with so many top artists appearing. Even the stars can't remain unexcited. After their set, Rob Halford of *Judas Priest* talks about the 'burst of wild energy' he got from being on stage.

The Wembley crowd are suddenly shown a live report from Ethiopia to remind them and the television viewers the principal reason for the concert. It's not just about music.

Paul Young comes on at Wembley and sings a verse of 'Do They Know It's Christmas?', followed by 'Come Back And Stay'. Then he welcomes his singing partner for the day, *Alison Moyet*. The new duo sing some old classics like 'That's The Way That Love Is'.

Bob Geldof comes on stage nearly bent double now and tells the Wembley audience to welcome the Philadelphia crowd, which flashes up on the screens. 72,000 people wave at a picture of 90,000 others waving back.

Autograph on video.

AUTOGRAPH

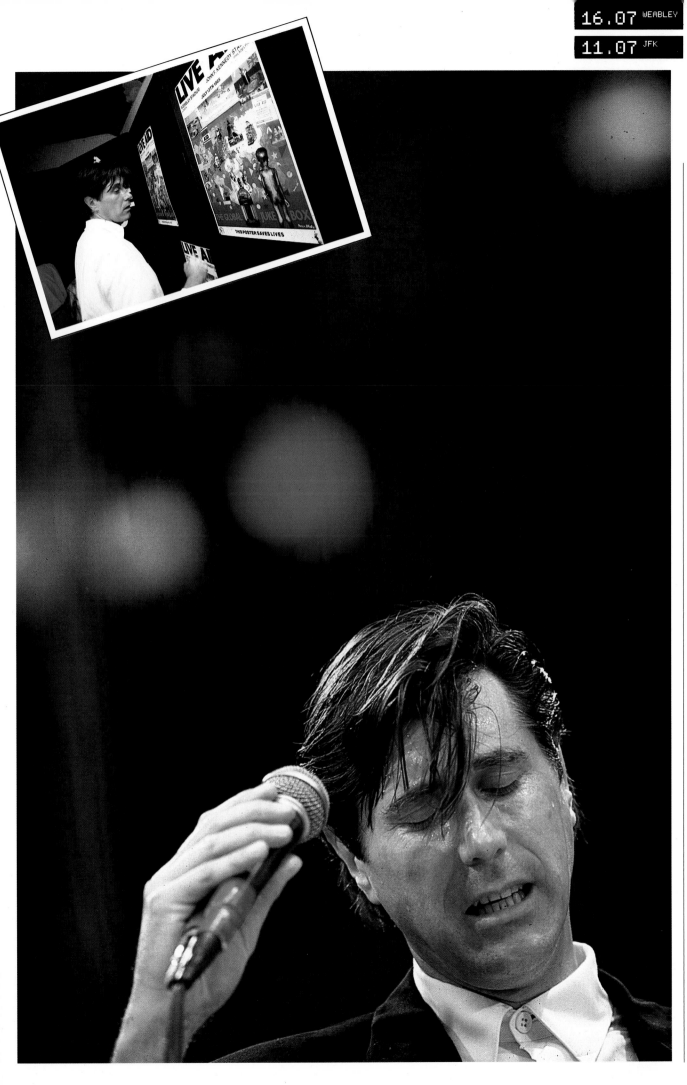

BRYAN FERRY

CROSBY, STILLS AND NASH

David Crosby, Graham Nash and Stephen Stills.

David Crosby.

Graham Nash.

Stephen Stills.

Rob Halford.

UDO LINDENBERG

Germany's Udo Lindenberg on video from Cologne.

The energy is there
simply because the
event creates such a
unique feeling –
Judas Priest

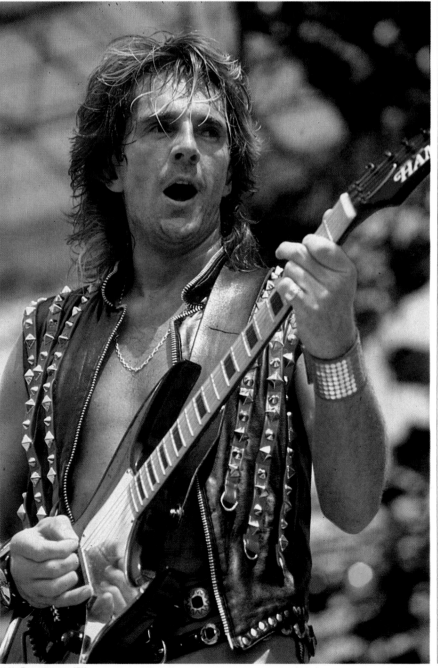

K.K. Downing at JFK.

PAUL YOUNG

If there's a problem, you
have to go out and solve
it – Bob Geldof

'Do They Know It's Christmas?' – Paul Young.

PAUL YOUNG/ALISON MOYET

Introducing Alison Moyet and Paul Young.

Police protection.

BOB GELDOF WELCOMES AMERICA

Bob Geldof and Paul Young.

Someone has counted this crowd, and it's 90,000.

Cool.

. . . one long party, with
people singing and
getting excited. We
knew something great
was going to happen –
Sharon Craig, 17

I'm just proud to be here. I'm a Canadian and tears are not enough. Let's all do what we can for Live Aid – Bryan Adams

Actor *Jack Nicholson* is introducing the acts in Philadelphia, and there's a massed squeal from the crowd as he mentions the name *Bryan Adams*. 'Everywhere I Go The Kids Just Want To Rock', and the dancing fans at JFK prove him right.

Jack Nicholson, from Philadelphia, then introduces *U2* in London. The group come on stage at Wembley, and the Irish singer, *Bono*, then leaves it. He jumps down among the crowd and grabs a girl and dances with her. Andy Warhol's statement about everyone being famous for 15 minutes is re-written – this girl is famous for 15 seconds as 1.5 billion people see her face. No one gets her name.

Then it's the turn of the *Beach Boys* in Philadelphia. Carl Wilson reckons that 'America has such an abundance of things that it should help people who haven't' and the group dishes out its traditional and abundant classics. Everyone at JFK is dancing, and so is everyone at Wembley, dancing at TV screens showing men 3,000 miles away singing songs written before some of them were born. Mick Brown wrote in *The Sunday Times*, 'One was aware of the eeriness of cities at opposite ends of the world waving at each other.'

Then, at Wembley, *Dire Straits* come on stage. They are playing another concert later that evening, but had to be here. They deliver a very tight set, and are joined by *Sting* who boogies with guitarist Mark Knopfler. Sting sings 'I Want My MTV' which understandably brings smiles to the faces of the MTV team backstage who are screening the whole thing.

Suddenly Bob Geldof lets loose and not because of his bad back. He's heard that the television appeals are slowing down. He yells at the television interviewer who is about to recite the address for donations: 'Fuck the address; give them the phone numbers.' We later learn that there was an astronomical upsurge in contributions. And in America, the phone computer broke down under the weight of 700,000 calls.

George Thorogood and The Destroyers appear in Philadelphia. They are joined by *Bo Diddley* and *Albert Collins*, steaming through a set of R and B classics. The Americans have issued 5,000 backstage passes. Some people are going out into the stadium, where it's less crowded.

Jack Nicholson.

'Tears Are Not Enough' is Canadian Bryan Adams' contribution to the USA For Africa fund-raising record.

Bono in custody.

U2

Bono.

U2

Bono makes his escape into the crowd...

... and finds a dancing partner.

New Dubliners.

THE BEACH BOYS

Brian Wilson.

They sound just the same.

DIRE STRAITS / STING

'The World's greatest guitarist today, Mark Knopfler' – Bob Geldof.

Sting with his band for the day... Dire Straits.

When can we do it again Bob?

This is what rock and
roll is all about. It's an
Event as much as it's
Music – Sting

GEORGE THOROGOOD AND THE DESTROYERS

Bo Diddley with George Thorogood.

George with blues legend Albert Collins.

George Thorogood.

We've had a complaint about the noise from the crowd – you aren't making enough – Comedian Mel Smith

Comedians *Mel Smith* and *Griff Rhys Jones* come on at Wembley, dressed as policemen, and harangue the crowd good-naturedly before introducing 'Her Majesty – *Queen*'. And on comes Freddie Mercury and the rest. Freddie sits at a piano and sings the opening words of 'Bohemian Rhapsody'; then he stops, jumps up and struts around the stage while the group break into 'Radio GaGa'. He then urges the crowd to sing 'Day-Oh', which they do. His vitality is awesome.

David Bowie, in London, and *Mick Jagger*, in Philadelphia, had planned to sing an intercontinental duet, but technical problems ruled it out. So they made a video together, instead. Both Wembley and Philadelphia watch Bowie and Jagger 'Dancing In The Street'. It is later reported that in some parts of Britain, young people left their television sets, and went out and, yes, danced in the streets, to the identical music pouring through every opened window.

Then a real-live Bowie comes on stage at Wembley, stylishly dressed in an ice-blue suit (oh, for some real ice, it's so hot) and sings his classics, 'Rebel, Rebel', 'Modern Love' and 'Heroes'. He leaves the stage flushed with excitement and emotion ('Let's do it again next year. Let's do it again every year'); then he comes back to tell the audience, 'You're the real heroes!'

Backstage, the stars seem to be greeting each other with a mixture of friendliness and shyness. 'I've just met Paul McCartney,' says Spandau Ballet's Tony Hadley, 'I worship him.' He refuses to say whether he asked for Paul's autograph, or whether it was just for his sister. Rock stars do not meet all that often. On this day, they're fans as well.

In Philadelphia, *Simple Minds* are on stage, and long before Jim Kerr gets to 'Don't You (Forget About Me)', everyone is singing along. Everyone marvels at the inexhaustible energy of the performers, but what about the energy of the fans? There are still hours to go, and nobody will leave.

Mel Smith and Griff Rhys-Jones.

Freddie Mercury.

QUEEN

John Deacon.

Brian May.

Roger Taylor.

Mick Jagger and David Bowie.

DAVID BOWIE/MICK JAGGER ON VIDEO

Joe Piscopo.

Simple Minds.

SIMPLE MINDS

Jim Kerr.

Simple Mind Jim Kerr.

DAVID BOWIE

The two-way drip feed of adrenalin between the performer on stage and the crowd out there is evident.

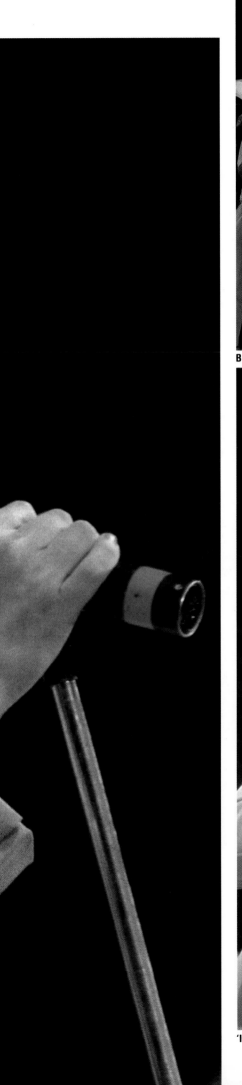

Bowie and his chorus line.

Bowie and Daltrey.

'I can't hear you, will you please sing up.'

...now we must give them a life – Bob Geldof

In between one of his exits, David Bowie introduces a specially made video about the famine in Africa. He decided at the last minute to drop one of his songs in favour of the video. A rock star without an ego? This day is certainly unique. After the noise, a sudden hush and stillness falls over Philadelphia and Wembley, and in millions of homes. More money is received at that moment than at any other point of the day.

In Philadelphia, Jim Kerr is replaced by his wife, Chrissie Hynde, and *The Pretenders*. These top groups usually play for, say, one or two hours, giving themselves time to build up. Here they have to come on cold, blasting solidly for 17 minutes. And there are some pretty hard acts to follow.

The Who are back, on stage together. They re-formed specially for Live Aid after three years of doing their own things. But it's clear that, although they've re-formed, they haven't reformed and still look as if they are about to smash guitars. Roger Daltrey went straight into 'My Generation' and it was almost as if the song was written a few days earlier. Pete Townshend did the splits in mid-air, just like he used to, and it really didn't matter that he fell over, it really didn't, not to 72,000 people at Wembley who roared their approval.

If they ask why...

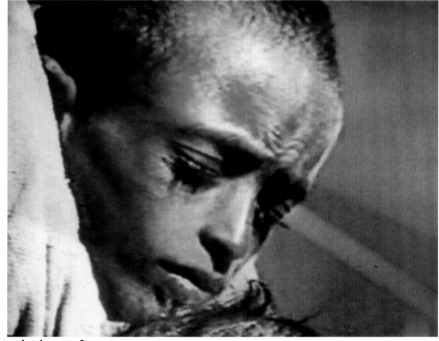

...what do we say?

130·LIVE AID

THE PRETENDERS

Chrissie Hynde.

With Jim Kerr.

We wanted people to
stop, to look, to listen
and most importantly to
help – The Pretenders

THE WHO

. . . it was rather like

getting one man's four

ex-wives together –

Bob Geldof on The Who

Pete Townshend.

Roger Daltrey.

Kenney Jones.

John Entwistle.

We always said we'd never play together again. We always meant it. But it would have been kind of difficult not to get together again for this day – Pete Townshend, The Who

The classic Pete Townshend leap.

> I wanted to do it, but I was very afraid. I was afraid for personal reasons. But at the same time we're trying to feed the hungry black children in Africa, and that takes on a whole new meaning for me – Teddy Pendergrass

SANTANA / PAT METHENY

Over in Philadelphia, another legendary group, *Santana*, perform their intoxicating blend of 'Latino-rock', and are joined in yet another impromptu jamming session by *Pat Metheny*. Everyone really does seem to be enjoying themselves today.

After a video from Norway of the country's Band Aid song, 'All Of Us', comedian *Billy Connolly* introduces Wembley 'to a friend of mine – *Elton John*'. Billy's friend comes on wearing a natty silk hat with a feather in it and a velvet smoking jacket (even in the heat, someone has to keep up dress standards – it can't always be left to Bryan Ferry). He takes his place at the piano and plays 'I'm Still Standing', 'Bennie And The Jets' and others from his long, long career. He then waves his hand and *Kiki Dee* comes on and they both sing their hit of nine years ago, 'Don't Go Breaking My Heart'.

Elton really seems to be reluctant to be on the stage alone, because he waves his hand again and *George Michael* comes on to sing his personal version of Elton's song, 'Don't Let The Sun Go Down'. He has formidable accompaniment – Elton John on piano and his partner in Wham! *Andy Ridgeley* as chorus.

After *Ashford & Simpson* in Philadelphia, the crowd grows quiet as a wheelchair comes on stage. Sitting in it is *Teddy Pendergrass*. It is extraordinarily moving; he hasn't performed in public since the car accident that left him a quadraplegic three years ago. But he had to perform for Live Aid. He is normally strapped into his wheelchair, but the leather straps are removed for his performance. He insists on sitting, and singing, unaided. His voice, weak at first, grows in strength and confidence and, at the end, tears streaming down his face, he is drowned out by the almighty roar from the crowd. It may be a long, hot day but everyone, tired or not, is on their feet, cheering. All the artists have crowded into their area to watch, and they're cheering, too.

Pat Metheny

Carlos Santana

138·LIVE AID

ELTON JOHN

Ashford and Simpson.

ASHFORD AND SIMPSON

One of the most moving moments: Teddy Pendergrass onstage for the first time since the car accident that left him paralysed.

Kiki Dee with Elton.

Andrew Ridgeley in the chorus line.

Kiki Dee.

ELTON JOHN / KIKI DEE

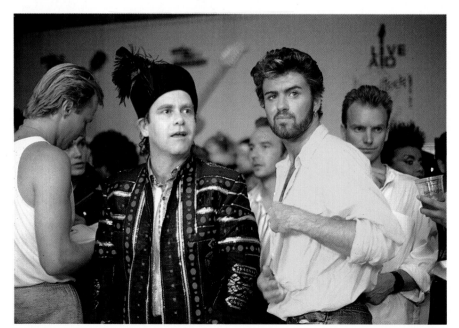

Stargaze.

George Michael.

WHAM!

I've just realized that today is the best day of my life. Now I'm going home to sleep – Bob Geldof

Bette Midler introducing Madonna.

In Philadelphia, *Bette Midler* introduces *Madonna* who dances around the stage as if it was a discotheque, and she is joined by the *Thompson Twins* and they all sing 'Love Makes The World Go Round', and the watching world loves it.

At Wembley, two chairs occupy the spotlight in the centre of the stage, and on come Queen's *Freddie Mercury* and *Brian May*, who quietly sing 'Is This The World We Created?'

Then the stage goes dark and from the darkness piano notes can be heard. The lights come on slowly and at the piano, so recently occupied by Elton John, sits *Paul McCartney*. For large numbers of the crowd it's the first time they've heard a Beatle sing a Beatles number, but nevertheless everyone knows the words to 'Let It Be', for when Paul's microphone briefly breaks down, they sing the words for him, to his piano.

As seems to be the custom, he raises his hand and beckons others on to the stage – and on walk Bob Geldof, Pete Townshend, Alison Moyet and David Bowie. Geldof was found fast asleep backstage at Wembley, and woken up. They make quite a respectable chorus, and could well have promising careers in music if they set their minds to it.

Five hands are then raised, and one hell of a chorus line walks on. It is the Finale at Wembley. Everyone who has been performing on this day comes on, no one has gone home. Some stars have even arrived. Cat Stevens, with a flowing beard to go with his flowing robes, turned up unannounced, and announced that he had written a special song, and could he play it? No, he couldn't, it was too late. It's chaotic and disorganized (Geldof tried to arrange a last-minute rehearsal, but it all fell apart), it's pure anarchy. But that's what makes it so wonderful, so moving, so memorable. People are crowded on to the stage, singing 'Do They Know It's Christmas?' Everyone in the crowd sings along too; it's noisy, it's moving, it's emotional. It's rock and roll. It's Live Aid. When they sing 'Feed The World', it is a shout of triumph, it is a command, it is a moral imperative. It is possible and today they have tried more than ever before to do just that. It is pop music's greatest moment. It rips through the hot night over Wembley and ripples off across the sound waves and around the planet. For Wembley Live Aid is over.

MADONNA

Freddie Mercury with Brian May.

MERCURY AND MAY

PAUL McCARTNEY

If the crowd want to hear 'Let it Be', I'll sing it.

Bowie and McCartney backstage.

David Bowie, Alison Moyet, Pete Townshend, Bob Geldof and Paul McCartney

FINALE

Finale, Wembley.

...and working to the very end, promoter Harvey Goldsmith. Finale, Wembley.

TOM PETTY

Two minutes before we came on stage, we decided to play 'American Girl', since this is, after all, JFK stadium, Philadelphia – Tom Petty

The fans stream out to get home and watch the rest of the show. The stars go to a London night club to watch the rest of the show. Because it's only tea time in Philadelphia, and there's still six hours more of Live Aid. *Tom Petty* and *Cars* play music from the West and East coasts of America – unmistakable and wonderful post-'76 American vintage. *Kenny Loggins* does his inimitable country rock, while in complete contrast *Neil Young* sings folk. The contrast is intentional – as Young explains backstage, 'The other groups are rock and roll, pounding out tunes that are keeping everyone up jumping. I'm doing the most laid-back act in the show. I only have one song that has a beat. All the other ones are slow.'

Power Station station themselves across the stage and pound out the music, keeping the audience moving round, under the giant hoses the firemen are helpfully using to keep people cool. The showers at the rear of the arena have long run out of water.

Tom Petty.

KENNY LOGGINS

Kenny Loggins.

Meanwhile, back at Wembley...

Rik Ocasek.

THE CARS

Elliot Easton and Benjamin Orr.

NEIL YOUNG

Neil Young.

Neil Young is joined by some old friends.

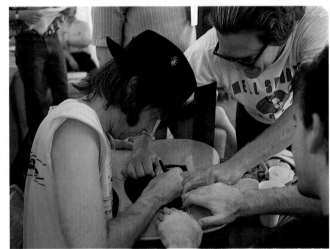

POWER STATION

Power Station's Michael Des Barres.

Andy Taylor.

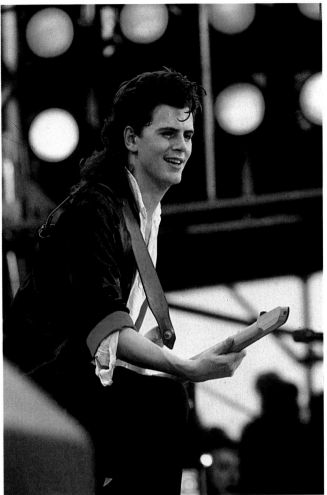

John Taylor.

Des Barres off-stage.

I wanted to be part of the
cause. When I take the
stage, my chance will
finally be here –
Tony Thompson,
Power Station

THE THOMPSON TWINS

I chose my songs for the show very carefully. I wanted music that would trace my development; I wanted to show my past and then my future, and also what I'm famous for – Eric Clapton

Today seems to be the day that everyone wants to do a bit more. The *Thompson Twins* come back on stage, and the diminutive figure singing backing vocals is *Madonna*.

You may remember, about eight hours ago, *Phil Collins* played at Wembley; well, here he is again, in Philadelphia, courtesy of Concorde. He plays 'Against All Odds', just like he did at Wembley, 'but I did it better here. I'm better in the evenings than the afternoon.'

But Phil still hasn't finished. Now he's the compere, introducing Led Zeppelin, *Jimmy Page, Robert Plant, John Paul Jones* with *Paul Martinez*. 'I'll tell you,' says Plant, 'there's no way you could have got these three guys together, if it wasn't for this cause.'

Now, Phil Collins dons yet another role, playing the drums as Led Zep goes into its anthem, 'Stairway To Heaven'. Nobody would have been surprised if Phil had suddenly come on stage again, grabbed *Eric Clapton*'s guitar and started playing that. He wouldn't have played it as well, of course, but would that necessarily have stopped him? He just didn't think of it.

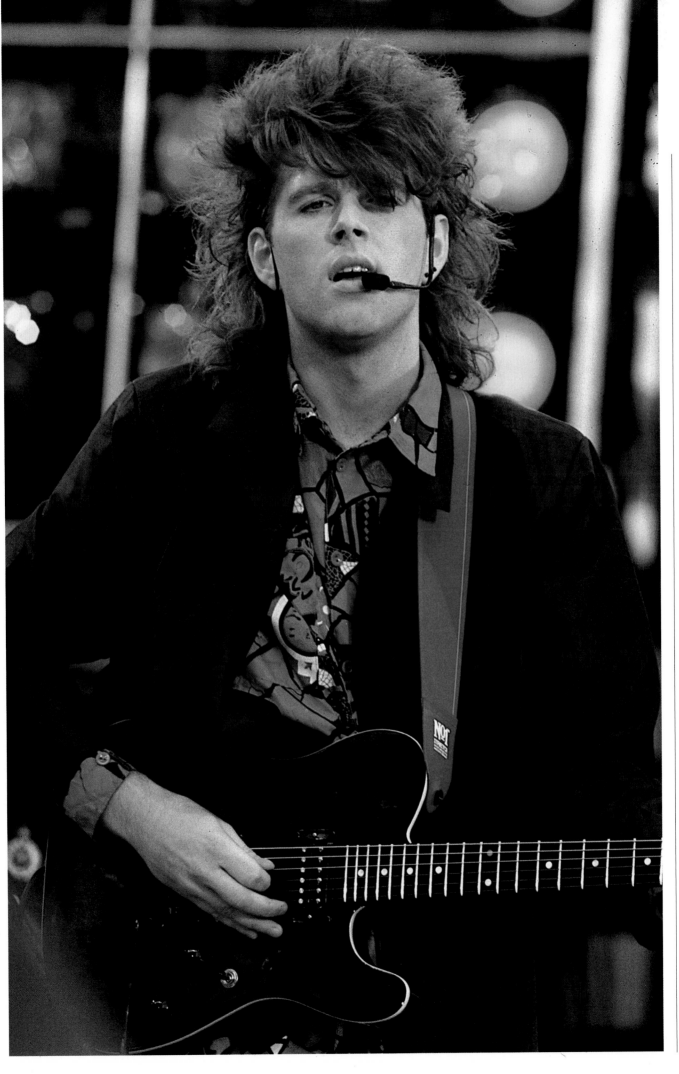

Slowhand.

ERIC CLAPTON

. . . momentum is unbelievable. You would have more trouble stopping it than putting it on – Eric Clapton

Phil leaves London.

...and arrives in Philadelphia.

I was in England this
afternoon . . . funny old
world innit –
Phil Collins

PHIL COLLINS

Phil Collins.

ROBERT PLANT / JIMMY PAGE / JOHN PAUL JONES

Robert Plant and Jimmy Page reunited.

John Paul Jones.

All these bands going on and no one's overrunning. That's a statement in itself – Jimmy Page

Relaxing backstage, Zep's Plant and Page.

What impresses me about today is that people who have a certain amount of sensitivity and artistic tendencies can be heard, and their music can make a difference – Daryl Hall

Duran Duran appear and launch into 'A View To A Kill', their current number one single.

They are followed by *Patti LaBelle*, and then by *Hall & Oates* (or it may have been the other way round; after 15 hours of non-stop rock and roll you get a little confused). They are joined by *Eddie Kendricks* and *Dave Ruffin* for some original Temptations songs – wonderful. For some unaccountable reason, Phil Collins is missing.

Back in London, a cheer has gone up in the night club which is throwing the party for the Live Aid stars (it also enables the BBC to continue interviewing people). This is not because of Collins' absence, but because of Cliff Richard's presence. He had been doing two charity concerts on the day, so couldn't make it to Live Aid. So he turned up at the club with a guitar, and sang into 'any ol' mike that's around'.

DURAN DURAN

I have been blessed in
my life and I don't take
my good fortune for
granted. That's what
Live Aid is all about –
Patti LaBelle

PATTI LABELLE

John Oates

Daryl Hall.

Hall, Oates, Ruffin and Kendricks.

HALL & OATES

They say the entertainment industry can never get together. Fooled them again, didn't we? – Dionne Warwick

MICK JAGGER

I came to play in Philadelphia because of the cause, because of Live Aid, of course. But I also came to have myself a good time. And I've sure as hell done that – Mick Jagger

Mick Jagger.

While David Bowie played in London, his video co-star *Mick Jagger* was in Philadelphia. He doesn't just come on stage, he gyrates on to it, his lips moving in time to his hips. He launches into 'Just Another Night'. And his backing group look familiar. It's Hall & Oates doing a bit more as well, watching as Mick covers the whole stage pointing fiercely at the audience, who don't seem at all frightened.

Then he puts a towel over his shoulders and yells 'All Right! Where's Tina?' and, in a slinky short dress, on comes *Tina Turner* (if it had been Phil Collins, now that would have been a blow). They sing and slink in perfect, er, harmony, through 'State Of Shock', a state shared by the audience, as Jagger removes first his shirt and then Tina's skirt.

Then Jack Nicholson, who's been there nearly all the long day, announces 'one of America's great voices of freedom'. The crowd don't have to be told the name – *Bob Dylan*. The tiny singer comes on stage with two guitarists with cigarettes hanging out of their mouths like gangsters in a French movie – the Rolling Stones' Ronnie Wood and Keith Richard.

Dylan sings his greatest songs, the 'Stones' play some laconic background sounds, and the penultimate act in the greatest concert line-up ever is finished.

And now for the final act. Dylan has been performing in front of a curtain. After he's gone off Lionel Ritchie comes on and sings the opening lines to 'We Are The World', and 90,000 voices in JFK pick up the words. The curtain opens, and a few other voices add their sounds. The stage is full with every act that had played in the stadium; plus some extra guests like Harry Belafonte, Sheena Easton and Cher. The stage is full of small children as well, adding their piping voices. It's been sort of rehearsed, but it all breaks down, like it should, in a riot of emotion.

It's 4 a.m. in London and the few survivors left in the night club silently mouth 'We Are The World' to the large TV screen. They hug each other, thank each other, then straggle out into the first light of Sunday. After 16 hours of the greatest day in pop history, the last band leaves the stage in Philadelphia one minute over time.

MICK JAGGER / TINA TURNER

MICK JAGGER/TINA TURNER

BOB DYLAN

It was the most electrifying feeling being there – no other reason than the cause. I wish I could do even more – Tina Turner

Ron Wood, Bob Dylan and Keith Richard.

Lionel Ritchie embraces Dylan.

LIONEL RITCHIE / FINALE

'We Are The World'. Finale, Philadelphia.

Dionne Warwick.

FINALE

Sheena Easton.

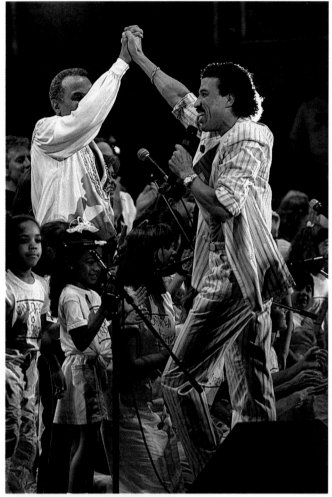

Harry Belafonte and Lionel Ritchie.

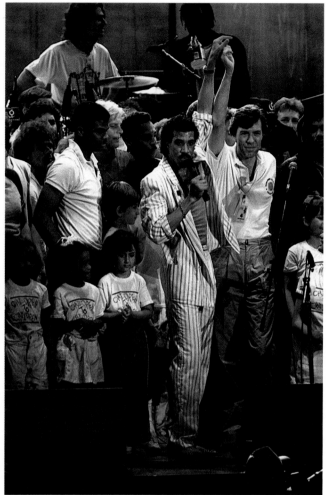

We are the children.

JFK Finale.

Acknowledgements

This book was written, designed, typeset and made ready for printing in 13 days. Printing and binding 100,000 copies took less than a week. This was made possible by the following individuals and organizations: Sally Welford; Roger Pring; Adrian Boot; Lynne Boot; Bob Christie; Miren Lopategui; Jenny de Gex; Bernard Doherty and Suki Pardesi of Rogers & Cowan, London; Alisha of Rogers & Cowan, New York; Graham Norris, Alan Ticehurst, Mike Jarvis and Peter Brealey of SX Composing; Optic Typesetting; Abacus Printing Co; John Price Studios; Face Photosetting; Conway Photosetting; BBB Design / Print; Roger Hawkins, Keith Allison, Dee Maple and Jenny of Graficas Espana Ltd; all the employees of Printer Industria Grafica Barcelona; Liza Lipkin and Deedee of Island Records; Lesley Bernstein; Caroleen Conquest; Ros Mair; Bill Tuesley, Paul Downes and Dean Crossman of WT Graphic Systems Ltd; Peter Seddon; Kevin Ryan; Graham Davis; Susan Hillmore; Lionel Rotcage; Kory Addis; Craig Blankenhorn; Sahm Doherty; Nick Flamini; Lidia Habeck; Sharon Halpern; Roman Iwasiwka; Sal DeMarco; Robert Partridge; Silvana Tharratt; Michael Marks; Jim Monteith; Ginger Stribula; Lancaster Labs Ltd; Syndication International; Steve Blogg; LGI; Leopold Cameras; Joe's Basement; All Action Photographic; Team Colour; Downtown Darkrooms; Retna Pictures; Alpha; Keith Johnson Photographic; Lancaster Colour; Kodak; Debby Walker; Carol Egerer; Michael Bialek; Clarence Mosley; John Enteman; Michael Ahern; the staff at Unicorn; Catherine Shuckburgh; Susan Hill; Nigel Newton; Jane Gregory; Duncan Paul; Harvey Goldsmith, John Kennedy, Judy Anderson and Kevin Jenden of the Band Aid Trust; Michael Appleton and Linda Langford of the BBC; Anne Furniss; Bob Geldof; Mary Smotry; Bill Bodie; Hal Uplinger; Tony Verna; Sidney D. Lovard; Bruce Higham; Anthea Doyle; Kushian Julburgh; Kerry Hood; Featherston Shipping; Chris Goldfinch; Varda Cohen and Arie Rosenfeld of Scitex.

Photo Credits
t: top, b: bottom, c: centre, l: left, r: right

Mohamed Amin 42t, 43, 48, 49; Brian Aris 30, 32, 35, 37b, 38, 39, 44-5; AT&T 56bl; Band Aid Trust 46-7; Adrian Boot 75, 77bl, 88t, 92, 95, 97, 98b, 113, 123tr, 123b, 130, 136, 140, 141, 144br, 156br, 158, 161, 167, 168, 170, 171t, 171c, 173, 174l, 175, 177, 178, 179, 180-1, 183, 184, 185, 186, 187, 188, 190-1; Laurence Bradbury 147b; British Telecom 56tl; Andrew Catlin 61t, 62b, 65, 69, 71, 73tl, 73r, 76, 78, 79b, 85, 93, 105, 109, 114, 119t, 133bl, 137, 138-9; Ann Clifford 16tc, 20cr; Allen Davidson 18br, 22tl, 22tr, 27cr, 61bl; Chalkie Davies 16cr, 50, 53b, 57, 60, 62t, 87, 121-2, 125r, 127tl, 132bl, 132br, 133tr, 146b, 150-1; Fox Keystone 22b, 66b; Mike Fuller (Camera 5) 189tl; Harrison Funk (Sipa Press) 19tl, 166b, 189; Frank Griffin 21bl, 115tl, 135, 142tl; Allen Grisbrooke 28tr, 29, 127tr; Bob Gruen 21t; John Hoffman 79t, 84, 86t, 103, 155b, 122, 127b, 132t, 152t; Dave Hogan 17b, 20b, 26cr, 102b, 108tl, 111r, 126, 142tr, 149bl; Nils Jorgenson 91, 110, 111tr, 118bl, 133tl, 133br, 139tl, 139tc, 139tr, 143; Barbara Kinney (USA Today) 74b, 77t, 80b, 82, 96, 98t, 99, 106r, 107, 124, 138tr, 144bl, 157, 159t, 160, 163t, 176b, 182; J. Langevin (Sygma) 111cr; Neil Leifer (Camera 5) 90, 152c; Kevin Mazur 18t, 55t, 163b; David McGough 16tr, 19tr, 23b, 26t, 27t, 27b, 59, 81t, 83b, 131, 144t, 156bl; Tony McGrath 40, 41; Paul Natkin 21br, 24br, 80tl, 88b, 89, 106l, 112, 156tr, 162, 166t, 174r, 176t; Denis O'Regan 24t, 24cl, 24cr, 26cl, 26br, 27c, 28b, 56br, 67, 68r, 72, 95t, 115 tr, 125l, 142br; Neal Preston (Camera 5) 16b, 64, 108bl, 149, 154-5; Duncan Raban 16tl, 17t, 17c, 20t, 22c, 27cl, 61br, 63, 68l, 72t, 100, 101, 102t, 118tr, 119br, 119bc, 119bl, 120tl, 120cl, 120bl, 134tl, 142cr; Steve Rapport 10-11, 51, 58, 70, 86b, 147t, 148cl, 153; Ken Regan (Camera 5) 12-13, 18bl, 23tl, 25, 28tl, 31, 33, 34, 36, 37t, 53t, 54t, 55b, 56tr, 74t, 81b, 104, 116, 117, 123tl, 169b, 172, 189tr; Rex Features 19c, 19b, 52; Ebet Roberts 20cl; Roy Williams 152b; Richard Young 26bl; Vinnie Zuffante 23tr, 169tr, 171b. Every effort has been made to credit all photographs accurately. We apologise for any errors or omissions.

Front cover photos by (clockwise from top left): David McGough; Duncan Raban; Jon Hoffman; Andrew Catlin; Steve Rapport; Chalkie Davies; Andrew Catlin; Duncan Raban; Neal Preston (Camera 5); Barbara Kinney (USA Today); Paul Natkin; Barbara Kinney (USA Today); Andrew Catlin; Adrian Boot; Mohamed Amin; Rex Features; Ken Regan (Camera 5); Adrian Boot; Rex Features; Adrian Boot; Harrison Funk (Sipa press); Dave Hogan; Adrian Boot; John Bellissimo (Retna Pictures).
Back cover photos by (clockwise from top left): David McGough; Adrian Boot; Adrian Boot; Alpha London; Steve Rapport; Ken Regan (Camera 5); Duncan Raban; Barbara Kinney (USA Today); Kevin Mazur; Barbara Kinney (USA Today); Rex Features; Andrew Catlin; Steve Rapport; Ebet Roberts; Adrian Boot; Andrew Catlin; Adrian Boot; Jon Hoffman; Duncan Raban; Duncan Raban; Andrew Catlin; Larry Busacca (Retna Pictures).